W9-BBN-067

DATE DUE

Jenni Fer

791.3   BC#34880000025978 $21.36
JOR   Jordan, Denise
         Welcome to the circus!

Morrill E.S.
Chicago Public Schools
1431 North Leamington Avenue
Chicago, IL 60651

Circus

Welcome to the Circus!

Denise M. Jordan

Heinemann Library
Chicago, Illinois

© 2002 Reed Educational & Professional Publishing
Published by Heinemann Library,
an imprint of Reed Educational & Professional Publishing,
Chicago, Illinois

Customer Service 888-454-2279
Visit our website at www.heinemannlibrary.com

Designed by Sue Emerson, Heinemann Library
Printed and bound in the U.S.A. by Lake Book

06 05
10 9 8 7 6 5 4 3

Library of Congress Cataloging-in-Publication Data
Jordan, Denise M.
    Welcome to the circus! / Denise Jordan.
        p. cm. — (Circus)
Includes index.
Summary: Briefly introduces the circus and circus performers.
    ISBN: 1-58810-541-5 (HC), 1-58810-749-3 (Pbk.)
    1. Circus—Juvenile literature. [1. Circus.] I. Title.
        GV1817 .J678 2002
        5791.3—dc21

                            2001004789

Acknowledgments
The author and publishers are grateful to the following for permission to reproduce copyright material:
p. 4 M. Lee/Trip; p. 5 Eugene G. Schulz; p. 6 Andre Jenny/Unicorn Stock Photos; p. 7 David June; p. 8 ChromoSohm/ Sohm/Unicorn Stock Photos; p. 9 Joel Dexter/Unicorn Stock Photos; p. 10 Steve Bourgeois/Unicorn Stock Photos; pp. 11, 21 Roland Raith; pp. 12, 13R, 14 Jane Faircloth/Transparencies, Inc.; p. 13L J. Moscrop/Trip; p. 15 Ken Deitcher; pp. 16, 20 Greg Williams/Heinemann Library; p. 17 S. Grant/Trip; p. 18 Craig Mitchelldyer; p. 19 Jeff Greenberg/Unicorn Stock Photos; p. 22 Robert Frerck/Odyssey/Chicago

Cover photograph courtesy of Robert Frerck/Odyssey/Chicago

Every effort has been made to contact copyright holders of any material reproduced in this book. Any omissions will be rectified in subsequent printings if notice is given to the publisher.

Special thanks to our advisory panel for their help in the preparation of this book:

Eileen Day, Preschool Teacher
Chicago, IL

Paula Fischer, K–1 Teacher
Indianapolis, IN

Sandra Gilbert,
Library Media Specialist
Houston, TX

Angela Leeper,
Educational Consultant
North Carolina Department
of Public Instruction
Raleigh, NC

Pam McDonald, Reading Teacher
Winter Springs, FL

Melinda Murphy,
Library Media Specialist
Houston, TX

Helen Rosenberg, MLS
Chicago, IL

Anna Marie Varakin,
Reading Instructor
Western Maryland College

The publishers would also like to thank Fred Dahlinger, Jr., Director of Collections and Research at the Circus World Museum in Baraboo, Wisconsin, and Smita Parida for their help in reviewing the contents of this book.

Some words are shown in bold, **like this.**
You can find them in the picture glossary on page 23.

Contents

What Is a Circus?

A circus is a big show.

A circus has animals, clowns, and **acrobats.**

People pay to see the circus.

Circuses move from town to town.

Where Are Circuses Held?

Some circuses are outside.

They are held in a tent called the **big top**.

Other circuses are inside large buildings.

What Happens at the Circus?

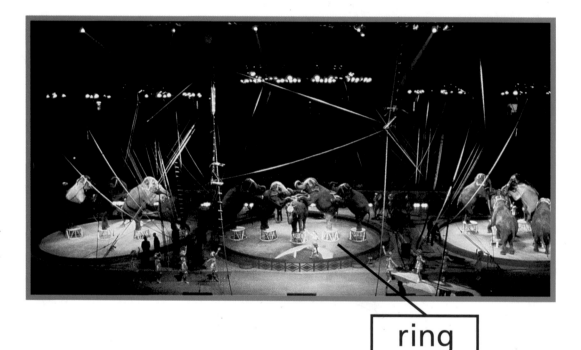

ring

Some circuses have three **rings** under the **big top**.

Different parts of the show are in each ring.

Some of the show is on
the ground.

Some is high in the air.

What Is a Ringmaster?

The **ringmaster** is the circus leader.

He stands inside the **ring**.

The ringmaster wears a jacket
and boots.

He tells people what they will see.

What Are Circus Performers?

Circus performers are people who do tricks.

Some are **acrobats**.

Other performers **tumble**.

Some performers walk on
a **tightrope**.

What Do Circus Animals Do?

Circus animals do tricks.

Circus lion and tiger acts
are exciting.

Circus dogs are like pets.

They can do funny tricks.

What Are Clowns?

Circus clowns make people laugh.

They paint their faces and wear funny clothes.

Clowns do silly things.

Some clowns work with animals.

What Do People Do at the Circus?

People watch the show at the circus.

They laugh at the clowns.

They are quiet when performers are working.

They cheer when the performers come down safely.

What Do People Eat at the Circus?

People eat cotton candy at the circus.

They eat hot dogs.

They eat popcorn, too.

Everything tastes good at the circus!

Quiz

Here are some things you can see at the circus.

Can you name them?

Look for the answers on page 24.

?

?

Picture Glossary

acrobat
pages 4, 12

ringmaster
pages 10, 11

big top
pages 6, 8

tightrope
page 13

ring
pages 8, 10

tumble
page 13

Note to Parents and Teachers

Reading for information is an important part of a child's literacy development. Learning begins with a question about something. Help children think of themselves as investigators and researchers by encouraging their questions about the world around them. Each chapter in this book begins with a question. Read the question together. Look at the pictures. Talk about what you think the answer might be. Then read the text to find out if your predictions were correct. Think of other questions you could ask about the topic, and discuss where you might find the answers. Assist children in using the picture glossary and the index to practice new vocabulary and research skills.

Index

Answers to quiz on page 22

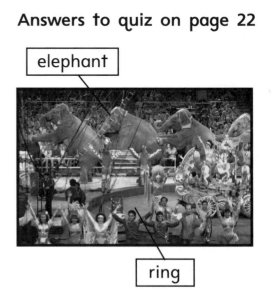

elephant

ring